Everyday Gourmet casseroles

Everyday Gourmet
casseroles

This edition published in 2010
LOVE FOOD is an imprint of Parragon Books Ltd

Parragon
Queen Street House
4 Queen Street
Bath BA1 1HE, UK

Introduction by Frances Eames
Photography by Don Last
Food Styling by Christine France

ISBN 978-1-4075-9444-6

Printed in China

Notes for the reader

- This book uses metric and imperial measurements. Follow the same units of measurement throughout; do not mix imperial and metric.
- All spoon measurements are level: teaspoons are assumed to be 5 ml and tablespoons are assumed to be 15 ml.
- Unless otherwise stated, milk is assumed to be semi-skimmed and eggs are medium. The times given are an approximate guide only.
- Some recipes contain nuts. If you are allergic to nuts you should avoid using them and any products containing nuts. Recipes using raw or very lightly cooked eggs should be avoided by infants, the elderly, pregnant women, convalescents and anyone suffering from illness.
- Vegans should be aware that some of the ready-made ingredients in the recipes in this book may be derived from animal products.
- Vegetarians should be aware that some of the ready-made ingredients in the recipes in this book may contain meat or meat products.

Contents

Introduction

Casseroles are the epitome of hearty, flavoursome cooking and make the perfect comfort food on a cold winter's day. Nourishing and easy to make, casseroles fit easily into a busy schedule, but produce meals that will make everyone smile.

The myth is that slow cooking is a lot of bother and takes too much time. In reality it doesn't take you any more time than other cooking; the only time needed is while the casserole sits happily all by itself in the oven, leaving the cook free to get on with other things.

The term 'casserole' is derived from the French for 'stew pan'. The culinary term *en casserole* means 'served in the vessel used for cooking' and refers to the ancient practice of stewing meat slowly in earthenware containers. Casseroles are cooked across the world from Europe to the United States, Africa to China.

Fuss-free

The joy of casseroles is that they are quick and easy to prepare, making them ideal for those of us with little time or inclination to prepare and cook labour-intensive meals. After a hard day at work, and the dark journey home on a winter's evening, there is nothing better than pulling a casserole from the fridge or freezer, placing it in the oven and relaxing until it's ready. And if you haven't had time to plan ahead, casseroles are still practical: just chop, fry, stir, and the rest of the cooking is done in the oven on its own. Preparation for casseroles has other advantages as it reduces the washing up, so you won't have to clean every pan in the house after dinner.

Diverse

Casserole recipes are no longer considered budget dishes. Although they are still economical and make

good sense for feeding families, the old image of casseroles has faded away. Casserole recipes are endlessly versatile, and contrary to what you may expect, there is a huge range of possible dishes. From Duck & Red Wine Casserole to Paella del Mar, casseroles offer a wide choice of flavours. They are also a great way to use up any left-overs in a tasty and practical way. On a cold winter's day casseroles are the perfect comfort food, a culinary hug for chilled children and hungry partners. But in summer when you don't fancy another salad, try Mediterranean inspired dishes such as Spanish Fish in Tomato Sauce or the exotic Moroccan Fish Tagine.

Nourishing

Casseroles are brimming with goodness, and are a great way to provide your family with healthy fare, without them noticing! In the age of 'five a day', you can be sure you're doing the best for them. Try to use vegetables that are in season to ensure you are getting the freshest ingredients, packed with vitamins. This also cuts down on your food's airmiles and your carbon footprint – you could even grow your own. It is best to use organic ingredients where possible and most supermarkets now offer organic options for a wide range of products.

Sociable entertaining

Far from being merely weekday meals, casseroles are actually perfect for entertaining. If you have been out with friends or family for the day, you just need to spend a few minutes to assemble the dish, pop it in the oven, and you can continue to chat and relax with everyone else. Casseroles are a great way to feed a hungry horde.

1

Meat Casseroles

serves 4

3 tbsp olive oil

2 onions, finely sliced

2 garlic cloves, chopped

1 kg/2 lb 4 oz good-quality braising steak

2 tbsp plain flour

300 ml/10 fl oz beef stock

bouquet garni sachet (shop-bought)

150 ml/5 fl oz full-bodied red wine

salt and pepper

1 tbsp chopped fresh parsley, to garnish

for the herb dumplings

115 g/4 oz self-raising flour, plus extra for shaping

55 g/2 oz suet

1 tsp mustard

1 tbsp chopped fresh parsley

1 tsp chopped fresh sage

4 tbsp cold water

stew & dumplings

Preheat the oven to 150°C/300°F/Gas Mark 2.

Heat 1 tablespoon of the oil in a large frying pan, add the onions and garlic and fry until softened and browned. Remove from the frying pan using a slotted spoon and place in a large casserole.

Trim the meat and cut into thick strips. Using the remaining oil, fry the meat in the frying pan over a high heat, stirring well until it is browned all over.

Sprinkle in the flour and stir well to prevent lumps. Season well with salt and pepper.

Pour in the stock, stirring constantly to make a smooth sauce, then continue to heat over a medium heat until the sauce is boiling.

Transfer the contents of the frying pan to the casserole.

Add the bouquet garni and the wine. Cover and cook in the centre of the oven for 2–2½ hours.

Begin making the dumplings about 25 minutes before the stew is ready. Sift the flour into a bowl, add the suet and the mustard and mix well. Stir in the herbs and then pour in enough of the water to form a firm but soft dough. Break the dough into 8 pieces and roll them into round dumplings (you might need some flour on your hands for this).

Remove the stew from the oven, check the seasoning, discard the bouquet garni and add the dumplings, pushing them down under the liquid. Cover and return the dish to the oven, continuing to cook for 20–25 minutes until the dumplings have doubled in size.

Serve the stew and dumplings piping hot with the parsley scattered over the top.

beef bourguignon

serves 4–6

- 85 g/3 oz butter
- 2 tbsp sunflower oil
- 175 g/6 oz smoked lardons, blanched for 30 seconds, drained and patted dry
- 900 g/2 lb stewing beef, such as chuck or leg
- 2 large garlic cloves, crushed
- 1 carrot, diced
- 1 leek, halved and sliced
- 1 onion, finely chopped
- 2 tbsp plain flour
- 350 ml/12 fl oz full-bodied red wine
- 500 ml/18 fl oz beef stock
- 1 tbsp tomato purée
- bouquet garni sachet (shop bought)
- 12 baby onions, peeled but kept whole
- 12 button mushrooms
- salt and pepper
- chopped fresh flat-leaf parsley, to garnish

Preheat the oven to 150°C/300°F/Gas Mark 2. Heat 25 g/1 oz of the butter and 1 tablespoon of the oil in a large, flameproof casserole. Cook the lardons over a medium-high heat, stirring, for 2 minutes, or until beginning to brown. Using a slotted spoon, remove from the casserole and drain on kitchen paper.

Trim the beef and cut it into 5-cm/2-inch chunks. Add the beef to the casserole and cook over a high heat, stirring frequently, for 5 minutes, or until browned on all sides and sealed, adding more of the butter or oil to the casserole as necessary. Using a slotted spoon, transfer the beef to a plate.

Pour off all but 2 tablespoons of the fat from the casserole. Add the garlic, carrot, leek and chopped onion and cook over a medium heat, stirring frequently, for 3 minutes, or until the onion is beginning to soften. Sprinkle in the flour, and salt and pepper to taste, and cook, stirring constantly, for 2 minutes, then remove the casserole from the heat.

Gradually stir in the wine and stock and add the tomato purée and bouquet garni, then return to the heat and bring to the boil, stirring and scraping any sediment from the base of the casserole.

Return the beef and lardons to the casserole and add extra stock if necessary so that the ingredients are covered by about 1 cm/½ inch of liquid. Slowly return to the boil, then cover and cook in the preheated oven for 2 hours.

Meanwhile, heat 25 g/1 oz of the remaining butter and the remaining oil in a large sauté pan or frying pan and cook the baby onions over a medium-high heat, stirring frequently, until golden all over. Using a slotted spoon, transfer the onions to a plate.

Heat the remaining butter in the pan and cook the mushrooms, with salt and pepper to taste, stirring frequently, until golden brown. Remove from the pan and then stir them, with the baby onions, into the casserole, re-cover and cook for a further 30 minutes, or until the beef is very tender.

Discard the bouquet garni, then adjust the seasoning to taste. Serve garnished with parsley.

beef & baby onion casserole

serves 6

- 2 tbsp olive oil
- 450 g/1 lb baby onions, peeled but kept whole
- 2 garlic cloves, halved
- 900 g/2 lb stewing beef, cubed
- 1/2 tsp ground cinnamon
- 1 tsp ground cloves
- 1 tsp ground cumin
- 2 tbsp tomato purée
- 750 ml/26 fl oz full-bodied red wine
- grated rind and juice of 1 orange
- 1 bay leaf
- salt and pepper
- 1 tbsp chopped fresh flat-leaf parsley, to garnish
- boiled or mashed potatoes, to serve

Preheat the oven to 150°C/300°F/Gas Mark 2. Heat the oil in a large, flameproof casserole and cook the whole onions and garlic, stirring frequently, for 5 minutes, or until softened and beginning to brown. Add the beef and cook over a high heat, stirring frequently, for 5 minutes, or until browned on all sides and sealed.

Stir the spices and tomato purée into the casserole and add salt and pepper to taste. Pour in the wine, scraping any sediment from the base of the casserole, then add the orange rind and juice and the bay leaf. Bring to the boil and cover.

Cook in the preheated oven for about 1 1/4 hours. Remove the lid and cook the casserole for a further hour, stirring once or twice, until the meat is tender. Remove from the oven, garnish with the parsley and serve hot, accompanied by boiled or mashed potatoes.

serves 4

450 g/1 lb lean boneless lamb, such as leg of lamb or fillet

1½ tbsp plain flour

1 tsp ground cloves

1–1½ tbsp olive oil

1 white onion, sliced

2–3 garlic cloves, sliced

300 ml/10 fl oz orange juice

150 ml/5 fl oz lamb stock or chicken stock

1 cinnamon stick, bruised

2 sweet (pointed, if available) red bell peppers, deseeded and sliced into rings

4 tomatoes

salt and pepper

few fresh sprigs coriander, plus 1 tbsp chopped fresh coriander, to garnish

lamb stew with sweet red peppers

Preheat the oven to 190°C/375°F/Gas Mark 5. Trim any fat or gristle from the lamb and cut into thin strips. Mix the flour and cloves together. Toss the lamb in the spiced flour until well coated and reserve any remaining spiced flour.

Heat 1 tablespoon of the oil in a heavy-based frying pan and cook the lamb over a high heat, stirring frequently, for 3 minutes, or until browned on all sides and sealed. Using a slotted spoon, transfer to an ovenproof casserole.

Add the onion and garlic to the frying pan and cook over a medium heat, stirring frequently, for 3 minutes, adding the extra oil if necessary. Sprinkle in the reserved spiced flour and cook, stirring constantly, for 2 minutes, then remove from the heat.

Gradually stir in the orange juice and stock, then return to the heat and bring to the boil, stirring.

Pour over the lamb in the casserole, add the cinnamon stick, red peppers, tomatoes and coriander sprigs and stir well. Cover and cook in the preheated oven for 1½ hours, or until the lamb is tender.

Discard the cinnamon stick and adjust the seasoning to taste. Serve garnished with the chopped coriander.

mediterranean lamb with apricots & pistachios

serves 4

- pinch of saffron threads
- 2 tbsp boiling water
- 450 g/1 lb lean boneless lamb, such as leg steaks
- 1½ tbsp plain flour
- 1 tsp ground coriander
- ½ tsp ground cumin
- ½ tsp ground allspice
- 1 tbsp olive oil
- 1 onion, chopped
- 2–3 garlic cloves, chopped
- 450 ml/16 fl oz lamb or chicken stock
- 1 cinnamon stick, bruised
- 85 g/3 oz dried apricots, roughly chopped
- 175 g/6 oz courgettes, sliced
- 115 g/4 oz cherry tomatoes
- 1 tbsp chopped fresh coriander
- salt and pepper
- 2 tbsp roughly chopped pistachio nuts, to garnish
- couscous, to serve

Put the saffron threads in a heatproof jug with the water and leave for at least 10 minutes to infuse. Trim off any fat or gristle from the lamb and cut into 2.5-cm/1-inch chunks. Mix the flour and spices together, then toss the lamb in the spiced flour until well coated and reserve any remaining spiced flour.

Heat the oil in a large, heavy-based saucepan and cook the onion and garlic, stirring frequently, for 5 minutes, or until softened. Add the lamb and cook over a high heat, stirring frequently, for 3 minutes, or until browned on all sides and sealed. Sprinkle in the reserved spiced flour and cook, stirring constantly, for 2 minutes, then remove from the heat.

Gradually stir in the stock and the saffron and its soaking liquid, then return to the heat and bring to the boil, stirring. Add the cinnamon stick and apricots. Reduce the heat, cover and simmer, stirring occasionally, for 1 hour.

Add the courgettes and tomatoes and cook for a further 15 minutes. Discard the cinnamon stick. Stir in the fresh coriander and season to taste with salt and pepper. Serve sprinkled with the pistachio nuts, accompanied by couscous.

serves 4

4 lamb shanks, about 350 g/ 12 oz each

6 garlic cloves

2 tbsp extra virgin olive oil

1 tbsp fresh rosemary, very finely chopped

salt and pepper

4 red onions

350 g/12 oz carrots, cut into thin batons

4 tbsp water

lamb shanks with roasted onions

Preheat the oven to 180°C/350°F/Gas Mark 4. Trim off any excess fat from the lamb shanks. Using a small, sharp knife, make 6 cuts in each lamb shank. Cut the garlic cloves lengthways into 4 slices. Insert 6 garlic slices into the cuts in each lamb shank.

Put the lamb in a single layer in a roasting tin, drizzle with the oil, sprinkle with the rosemary and season to taste with pepper. Roast in the preheated oven for 45 minutes.

Wrap each of the onions in a piece of foil. Remove the roasting tin from the oven and season the lamb to taste with salt. Return to the oven and put the wrapped onions on the shelf next to it. Roast for a further 1–1¼ hours until the lamb is very tender. Meanwhile, bring a large saucepan of water to the boil. Add the carrot batons and blanch for 1 minute. Drain and refresh in cold water.

Remove the roasting tin from the oven when the lamb is meltingly tender and transfer to a warmed serving dish. Skim off any fat from the roasting tin and put the tin over a medium heat. Add the carrots and cook, stirring, for 2 minutes, then add the water and bring to the boil. Reduce the heat and simmer, stirring constantly and scraping any sediment from the base of the tin.

Transfer the carrots and sauce to the serving dish. Remove the onions from the oven and unwrap. Cut off and discard about 1 cm/½ inch of the tops and add the onions to the serving dish. Serve immediately.

pork stroganoff

serves 4

- 350 g/12 oz lean pork fillet
- 1 tbsp vegetable oil
- 1 medium onion, chopped
- 2 garlic cloves, crushed
- 25 g/1 oz plain flour
- 2 tbsp tomato purée
- 425 ml/15 fl oz chicken or vegetable stock
- 125 g/4½ oz button mushrooms, sliced
- 1 large green pepper, deseeded and chopped
- ½ tsp freshly grated nutmeg, plus extra to garnish
- 4 tbsp low-fat natural yogurt, plus extra to serve
- salt and pepper
- boiled rice with chopped fresh parsley, to serve

Trim off any fat or gristle from the pork and cut into 1-cm/½-inch thick slices. Heat the vegetable oil in a large, heavy-based frying pan and gently fry the pork, onion and garlic for 4–5 minutes, or until lightly browned.

Stir in the flour and tomato purée, then pour in the chicken stock and stir to mix thoroughly. Add the mushrooms, pepper, salt and pepper to taste and nutmeg. Bring to the boil, cover and simmer for 20 minutes, or until the pork is tender and cooked through.

Remove the frying pan from the heat and stir in the yogurt. Transfer the pork to 4 large, warmed serving plates and serve with boiled rice sprinkled with chopped fresh parsley and an extra spoonful of yogurt, garnished with freshly grated nutmeg.

serves 4

- 450 g/1 lb lean pork fillet
- 1½ tbsp plain flour
- 1 tsp ground coriander
- 1 tsp ground cumin
- 1½ tsp ground cinnamon
- 1 tbsp olive oil
- 1 onion, chopped
- 400 g/14 oz canned chopped tomatoes
- 2 tbsp tomato purée
- 300–450 ml/10–16 fl oz chicken stock
- 225 g/8 oz carrots, chopped
- 350 g/12 oz squash, such as kabocha, peeled, deseeded and chopped
- 225 g/8 oz leeks, sliced, blanched and drained
- 115 g/4 oz okra, trimmed and sliced
- salt and pepper
- sprigs of fresh parsley, to garnish
- couscous, to serve

pork & vegetable stew

Trim off any fat or gristle from the pork and cut into thin strips about 5 cm/2 inches long. Mix the flour and spices together. Toss the pork in the spiced flour until well coated and reserve any remaining spiced flour.

Heat the oil in a large, heavy-based saucepan and cook the onion, stirring frequently, for 5 minutes, or until softened. Add the pork and cook over a high heat, stirring frequently, for 5 minutes, or until browned on all sides and sealed. Sprinkle in the reserved spiced flour and cook, stirring constantly, for 2 minutes, then remove from the heat.

Gradually add the tomatoes to the saucepan. Blend the tomato purée with a little of the stock in a jug and gradually stir into the saucepan, then stir in half the remaining stock.

Add the carrots, then return to the heat and bring to the boil, stirring. Reduce the heat, cover and simmer, stirring occasionally, for 1½ hours. Add the squash and cook for a further 15 minutes.

Add the leeks and okra, and the remaining stock if you prefer a thinner stew. Simmer for a further 15 minutes, or until the pork and vegetables are tender. Season to taste with salt and pepper, then garnish with fresh parsley and serve with couscous.

ham with black-eyed beans

serves 4

- 450–550 g/1–1 lb 4 oz lean gammon
- 2½ tbsp olive oil, plus 1–2 tsp
- 1 onion, chopped
- 2–3 garlic cloves, chopped
- 2 celery sticks, chopped
- 175 g/6 oz sliced carrots
- 1 cinnamon stick, bruised
- ½ tsp ground cloves
- ¼ tsp freshly grated nutmeg
- pepper
- 1 orange pepper
- 1 tsp dried oregano
- 450 ml/16 fl oz chicken stock or vegetable stock
- 1–2 tbsp maple syrup
- 3 large spicy sausages, or about 225 g/8 oz chorizo
- 400 g/14 oz canned black-eyed beans or broad beans
- 1 tbsp cornflour

Trim off any fat or skin from the gammon and cut into 4-cm/1½-inch chunks. Heat 1 tablespoon oil in a heavy-based saucepan or flame-proof casserole and cook the gammon over a high heat, stirring frequently, for 5 minutes, or until browned on all sides and sealed. Using a slotted spoon, remove from the saucepan and set aside.

Add the onion, garlic, celery and carrots to the saucepan with a further 1 tablespoon oil and cook over a medium heat, stirring frequently, for 5 minutes, or until softened. Add all the spices, season with pepper to taste, and cook, stirring constantly, for 2 minutes.

Return the gammon to the saucepan. Add the dried oregano, stock, and maple syrup to taste, then bring to the boil, stirring. Reduce the heat, cover and simmer, stirring occasionally, for 1 hour.

Heat the remaining ½ tablespoon oil in a frying pan and cook the sausages, turning frequently, until browned all over. Remove and cut each into 3–4 chunks, then add to the saucepan. Drain and rinse the beans, then drain again. Deseed and chop the orange pepper. Add the beans and pepper to the pan, and simmer for a further 20 minutes. Blend 2 tablespoons of water with the cornflour and stir into the stew, then cook for 3–5 minutes. Discard the cinnamon stick and serve immediately.

pork casserole

serves 6

- 85 g/3 oz plain flour
- 1.3 kg/3 lb lean pork fillet, cut into 5-mm/1/4-inch slices
- 4 tbsp sunflower oil
- 2 onions, thinly sliced
- 2 garlic cloves, finely chopped
- 400 g/14 oz canned chopped tomatoes in juice
- 350 ml/12 fl oz dry white wine
- 1 tbsp torn fresh basil leaves
- 2 tbsp chopped fresh parsley, plus extra sprigs to garnish
- salt and pepper
- fresh crusty bread, to serve

Spread the flour out on a plate and season to taste with salt and pepper. Trim off any fat or gristle from the pork and cut into 5-mm/1/4-inch thick slices. Toss the pork slices in the flour to coat, shaking off any excess. Heat the oil in a flameproof casserole over a medium heat. Add the pork slices and cook until browned all over. Using a slotted spoon, transfer the pork to a plate.

Add the onions to the casserole and cook over a low heat, stirring occasionally, for 10 minutes, or until golden brown. Add the garlic and cook, stirring, for 2 minutes, then add the tomatoes with their juice, the wine and basil leaves and season to taste with salt and pepper. Cook, stirring frequently, for 3 minutes.

Return the pork to the casserole, cover and simmer gently for 1 hour, or until the meat is tender. Stir in the chopped parsley. Serve immediately, garnished with parsley sprigs and accompanied by fresh crusty bread.

2

Poultry & Game Casseroles

serves 4

- 2 tbsp butter
- 8 baby onions
- 125 g/4½ oz streaky bacon, roughly chopped
- 4 chicken joints
- 1 garlic clove, finely chopped
- 12 button mushrooms
- 300 ml/10 fl oz full-bodied red wine
- bouquet garni sachet (shop-bought)
- 1 tbsp chopped fresh tarragon
- 2 tsp cornflour
- 1–2 tbsp cold water
- salt and pepper
- chopped flat-leaf parsley, to garnish

coq au vin

Melt half of the butter in a large frying pan over a medium heat. Add the onions and bacon and cook, stirring, for 3 minutes. Lift out the bacon and onions and reserve.

Melt the remaining butter in the frying pan and add the chicken joints. Cook for 3 minutes, then turn over and cook on the other side for 2 minutes. Drain off some of the chicken fat before returning the bacon and onions to the pan. Then add the garlic, mushrooms, red wine, bouquet garni and tarragon. Season to taste with salt and pepper. Cook for about 1 hour, or until the chicken is cooked through.

Remove the frying pan from the heat, lift out the chicken, onions, bacon and mushrooms, transfer them to a serving platter and keep warm. Discard the bouquet garni.

Mix the cornflour with enough of the water to make a paste, then stir into the juices in the frying pan. Bring to the boil, reduce the heat and cook, stirring, for 1 minute. Pour the sauce over the chicken and serve garnished with the chopped parsley.

serves 4

1½ tbsp unsalted butter

2 tbsp olive oil

450 kg/4 lb skinned chicken drumsticks

2 red onions, sliced

2 garlic gloves, chopped finely

400 g/14 oz canned chopped tomatoes

2 tbsp chopped flat-leaf parsley, plus extra for garnish

6 fresh basil leaves, torn

1 tbsp sun-dried tomato purée

150 ml/5 fl oz full-bodied red wine

225 g/8 oz mushrooms, sliced

salt and pepper

chicken, tomato & onion casserole

Preheat the oven to 160°C/325°F/Gas Mark 3.

Heat the butter with the olive oil in a large, ovenproof casserole. Add the chicken drumsticks and cook, turning frequently, for 5–10 minutes, or until golden all over and sealed. Using a slotted spoon, transfer the drumsticks to a plate.

Add the onions and garlic to the casserole and cook over low heat, stirring occasionally, for 10 minutes, or until golden. Add the tomatoes and the juices from the can, the parsley, basil, tomato purée and wine, and season to taste with salt and pepper. Bring to the boil, then return the chicken drumsticks to the casserole, pushing them down under the liquid.

Cover and cook in the oven for 50 minutes. Add the mushrooms and cook for a further 10 minutes, or until the chicken drumsticks are tender and the juices run clear when a skewer is inserted in to the thickest part of the meat. Serve immediately garnished with chopped parsley.

chicken & apple pot

serves 4

- 4 chicken portions, about 150 g/5 1/2 oz each, skinned if preferred
- 1 tbsp olive oil
- 1 onion, chopped
- 2 celery sticks, roughly chopped
- 1 1/2 tbsp plain flour
- 300 ml/10 fl oz clear apple juice
- 150 ml/5 fl oz chicken stock
- 1 cooking apple, cored and quartered
- 2 bay leaves
- 1–2 tsp clear honey
- 1 yellow pepper, deseeded and cut into chunks
- 1 tbsp butter
- 1 large or 2 medium eating apples, cored and sliced
- 2 tbsp demerara sugar
- salt and pepper
- 1 tbsp chopped fresh mint, to garnish

Preheat the oven to 190°C/375°F/Gas Mark 5. Lightly rinse the chicken and pat dry with kitchen paper.

Heat the oil in a deep frying pan and cook the chicken over a medium-high heat, turning frequently, for 10 minutes, or until golden all over and sealed. Using a slotted spoon, transfer to an ovenproof casserole.

Add the onion and celery to the frying pan and cook over a medium heat, stirring frequently, for 5 minutes, or until softened. Sprinkle in the flour and cook, stirring constantly, for 2 minutes, then remove from the heat.

Gradually stir in the apple juice and stock, then return to the heat and bring to the boil, stirring. Add the cooking apple, bay leaves, and honey and season to taste.

Pour over the chicken in the casserole, cover and cook in the preheated oven for 25 minutes. Add the yellow pepper and cook for a further 10–15 minutes, or until the chicken is tender and the juices run clear when a skewer is inserted into the thickest part of the meat.

Meanwhile, preheat the grill to high. Melt the butter in a saucepan over a low heat. Line the grill pan with kitchen foil. Brush the eating apple slices with half the butter, sprinkle with a little sugar and cook under the grill for 2–3 minutes, or until the sugar has caramelized. Turn the slices over, brush with the remaining butter and sprinkle with the remaining sugar, then cook for a further 2 minutes. Serve the stew garnished with the mint and caramelized apple slices.

garlic chicken casserole

serves 4

- 4 tbsp sunflower oil
- 900 g/2 lb chicken meat, chopped
- 250 g/9 oz mushrooms, sliced
- 16 shallots
- 6 garlic cloves, crushed
- 1 tbsp plain flour
- 250 ml/9 fl oz dry white wine
- 250 ml/9 fl oz chicken stock
- 1 fresh bouquet garni with sage
- 1 celery stick
- salt and pepper
- 400 g/14 oz canned borlotti beans, drained and rinsed
- steamed squash, to serve

Preheat the oven to 150°C/300°F/Gas Mark 2.

Heat the sunflower oil in an ovenproof casserole and fry the chicken until browned all over. Using a slotted spoon remove the chicken from the casserole and set aside until required.

Add the mushrooms, shallots and garlic to the casserole and cook for 4 minutes.

Return the chicken to the casserole and sprinkle with the flour, then cook for a further 2 minutes.

Add the white wine and chicken stock, stir until boiling, then add the bouquet garni and celery stick. Season with salt and pepper to taste.

Add the beans to the casserole.

Cover and place in the centre of the oven and cook for 2 hours. Remove the bouquet garni and celery stick and serve the casserole with steamed squash.

chicken, pumpkin & chorizo casserole

serves 4

- 3 tbsp olive oil
- 5 lb/2.25 kg chicken, cut into 8 pieces and dusted in flour
- 200 g/7 oz fresh chorizo sausages, roughly sliced
- small bunch of sage leaves
- 1 onion, chopped
- 6 cloves garlic, sliced
- 2 sticks celery, sliced
- 1 small pumpkin/butternut squash, peeled and roughly chopped
- 200 ml/7 fl oz dry sherry
- 600 ml/1 pint chicken stock
- 400 g/14 oz chopped tomatoes
- 2 bay leaves
- salt and pepper
- 1 tbsp chopped fresh flat-leaf parsley

Preheat the oven to 180°C/350°F/Gas Mark 4.

Fry the chicken in the olive oil in a casserole with the chorizo and sage leaves, until golden brown. Remove with a slotted spoon and reserve. You may need to do this in two batches.

Add the onion, garlic, celery and pumpkin to the casserole and cook for 20 minutes or until the mixture is golden brown.

Add the sherry, chicken stock, tomatoes and bay leaves, and season with salt and pepper.

Add the reserved chicken, chorizo and sage back into the casserole dish.

Cover with a lid and cook in the oven for one hour.

Remove from oven, stir in the chopped parsley and serve.

chicken casserole with a herb crust

serves 4

- 4 whole chicken legs, dusted in flour
- 1 tbsp olive oil
- 1 tbsp butter
- 1 onion, chopped
- 3 cloves garlic, sliced
- 4 parsnips, peeled and cut into large chunks
- 150 ml/5 fl oz dry white wine
- 900 ml/1½ pint chicken stock
- 3 leeks, white parts only, sliced
- 75 g/3 oz prunes, halved (optional)
- 1 tbsp English mustard
- bouquet garni sachet (shop bought)
- 100 g/4 oz fresh breadcrumbs
- 75 g/3 oz Caerphilly cheese, crumbled
- salt and pepper
- 50 g/2 oz mixed chopped tarragon and flat-leaf parsley

Preheat oven to 180°C/350°F/Gas Mark 4.

Fry the chicken in a casserole with the olive oil and butter, until golden brown. Remove with a slotted spoon and keep warm.

Add the onion, garlic and parsnips to the casserole and cook for 20 minutes or until the mixture is golden brown.

Add the wine, stock, leeks, prunes (if using), English mustard and bouquet garni and season with salt and pepper.

Add the chicken to the casserole, place on the lid and cook in the oven for 1 hour. Meanwhile mix together the breadcrumbs, cheese and herbs.

Remove the casserole from the oven and increase the heat to 200°C/400°F/Gas Mark 6.

Remove the lid of the casserole and sprinkle over the crust mixture. Return to the oven for 10 minutes, uncovered, until the crust starts to brown slightly.

Remove from the oven and serve.

duckling with lentils

serves 4

1 duckling, weighing 2.25 kg/5 lb

225 g/8 oz small brown lentils

1 tbsp virgin olive oil

2 onions

2 celery sticks

2 tbsp brandy or grappa

150 ml/5 fl oz dry white wine

1 tsp cornflour

salt and pepper

for the stock

wings, backbone and neck from the duckling

1 celery stick

1 garlic clove

6 peppercorns, lightly crushed

1 bay leaf

5 fresh flat-leaf parsley sprigs

1 onion

1 clove

large pinch of salt

Cut the duckling into joints. Cut off the wings. Fold back the skin at the neck end and cut out the wishbone with a small, sharp knife. Using poultry shears or heavy kitchen scissors, cut the breast in half along the breastbone, from the tail end to the neck. Cut along each side of the backbone to separate the 2 halves. Remove the backbone. Cut each portion in half diagonally.

To make the stock, put the wings, backbone and neck, if available, in a large saucepan and add the celery, garlic, peppercorns, bay leaf and parsley. Stick the onion with the clove and add to the saucepan with the salt. Add cold water to cover and bring to the boil. Skim off any scum that rises to the surface, then reduce the heat and simmer very gently for 2 hours. Strain into a clean saucepan and boil until reduced and concentrated. Reserve the stock, keeping 150 ml/5fl oz separate from the rest.

Rinse the lentils and place in a saucepan. Add the oil and cold water to cover. Halve one of the onions and add to the saucepan with one celery stick. Bring to the boil, then simmer for 15 minutes, or until the lentils have softened. Drain and set aside.

Meanwhile, add the ducking pieces, skin-side down, in a frying pan and cook for 10 minutes. Transfer to an ovenproof casserole and drain off any excess fat.

Finely chop the remaining onions and celery and add to the frying pan. Cook over a low heat, stirring occasionally, for 5 minutes, until softened. Using a slotted spoon, transfer the vegetables to the casserole.

Cook the casserole over medium heat, add the brandy and ignite. When the flames have died down, add the wine and reserved stock less 2 tablespoons. Bring to the boil, add the lentils, salt and pepper. Cover and simmer over low heat for 40 minutes, or until the lentils and duck are tender.

In a small bowl, blend the cornflour to a smooth paste with 2 tbsp of the remaining reserved stock. Stir the paste into the casserole and cook, stirring constantly, for 5 minutes, or until thickened. Add salt to taste and adjust the seasoning, if necessary. Serve immediately.

serves 4

- 4 duck portions, about 150 g/5$^1/_2$ oz each
- 1–2 tsp olive oil, plus 1 tbsp (optional)
- 1 red onion, cut into wedges
- 2–3 garlic cloves, chopped
- 1 large carrot, chopped
- 2 celery sticks, chopped
- 2 tbsp plain flour
- 300 ml/10 fl oz full-bodied red wine
- 2 tbsp brandy (optional)
- 150–200 ml/5–7 fl oz stock or water
- 7.5-cm/3-inch strip of orange rind
- 2 tsp redcurrant jelly
- 115 g/4 oz sugarsnap peas
- 115 g/4 oz button mushrooms
- salt and pepper
- 1 tbsp chopped fresh parsley, to garnish

duck & red wine casserole

Remove and discard the fat from the duck. Lightly rinse and pat dry with kitchen paper.

Heat a large, deep frying pan for 1 minute until warm but not piping hot. Put the duck portions in the frying pan and heat gently until the fat starts to run. Increase the heat a little, then cook, turning over halfway through, for 5 minutes, or until browned on both sides and sealed. Using a slotted spoon, transfer to a flameproof casserole.

Add 1 tablespoon of the oil if there is little duck fat in the frying pan and cook the onion, garlic, carrot and celery, stirring frequently, for 5 minutes, or until softened. Sprinkle in the flour and cook, stirring constantly, for 2 minutes, then remove the frying pan from the heat.

Gradually stir in the wine, brandy (if using), and stock, then return to the heat and bring to the boil, stirring. Season to taste with salt and pepper, then add the orange rind and redcurrant jelly. Pour over the duck portions in the casserole, cover and simmer, stirring occasionally, for 1–1$^1/_4$ hours.

Cook the sugarsnap peas in a saucepan of boiling water for 3 minutes, then drain and add to the stew. Meanwhile, heat 1–2 teaspoons of the olive oil in a small saucepan and cook the mushrooms, stirring frequently, for 3 minutes, or until beginning to soften. Add to the stew. Cook the stew for a further 5 minutes, or until the duck is tender. Serve garnished with the parsley.

serves 4

- 4 duck breasts, about 150 g/5½ oz each
- 2 tbsp olive oil
- 225 g/8 oz piece gammon, cut into small chunks
- 225 g/8 oz chorizo, outer casing removed
- 1 onion, chopped
- 3 garlic cloves, chopped
- 3 celery sticks, chopped
- 1–2 fresh red chillies, deseeded and chopped
- 1 green pepper, deseeded and chopped
- 600 ml/1 pint chicken stock
- 1 tbsp chopped fresh oregano
- 400 g/14 oz canned chopped tomatoes
- 1–2 tsp hot pepper sauce, or to taste
- 225 g/8 oz long-grain rice
- fresh sprigs of parsley, to garnish
- green salad and freshly cooked long-grain rice, to serve

duck jambalaya-style stew

Remove and discard the skin and any fat from the duck breasts. Cut the flesh into bite-sized pieces.

Heat half the oil in a large deep frying pan and cook the duck, gammon and chorizo over a high heat, stirring frequently, for 5 minutes, or until browned on all sides and sealed. Using a slotted spoon, remove from the frying pan and set aside.

Add the onion, garlic, celery and chilli to the frying pan and cook over a medium heat, stirring frequently, for 5 minutes, or until softened. Add the green pepper, then stir in the stock, oregano, tomatoes and hot pepper sauce.

Bring to the boil, then reduce the heat and return the duck, gammon and chorizo to the frying pan. Cover and simmer, stirring occasionally, for 20 minutes, or until the duck and gammon are tender.

Drain and serve, garnished with parsley and accompanied by a green salad and rice.

venison casserole

serves 6

- 3 tbsp olive oil
- 1 kg/2 lb 4 oz casserole venison, cut into 3-cm/ 1¼-inch cubes
- 2 onions, peeled and finely sliced
- 2 garlic cloves, peeled and chopped
- 350 ml/12 fl oz beef or vegetable stock
- 2 tbsp plain flour
- 125 ml/4 fl oz port or full-bodied red wine
- 2 tbsp redcurrant jelly
- 6 juniper berries, crushed
- 4 cloves, crushed
- pinch of cinnamon
- small grating of nutmeg
- salt and pepper
- baked or mashed potatoes, to serve

Preheat the oven to 180°C/350°F/Gas 4. Heat the oil in a large frying pan and cook the cubes of venison over a high heat for 2–3 minutes until brown. You may need to fry the meat in two or three batches – do not overcrowd the pan. Remove the venison from the pan using a slotted spoon and place in the casserole dish.

Add the onion and garlic to the pan and fry over a medium heat for about 3 minutes until a good golden colour, then lift out and add to the meat.

Gradually add the stock to the frying pan, stir well and scrape up the sediment, then bring to the boil.

Sprinkle the meat in the casserole dish with the flour and turn to coat evenly.

Add the hot stock to the casserole and stir well, ensuring that the meat is just covered.

Add the wine, redcurrant jelly and the spices.

Season well, cover and cook gently in the centre of the preheated oven for 2–2½ hours.

Remove from the oven, check the seasoning and adjust if necessary. Serve immediately piping hot with baked or mashed potatoes.

3

Fish & Seafood Casseroles

seafood stew

serves 4

- 1 yellow pepper, 1 red pepper, 1 orange pepper, deseeded and quartered
- 450 g/1 lb ripe tomatoes
- 2 large, fresh, mild green chillies, such as poblano
- 6 garlic cloves, peeled but kept whole
- 2 tsp dried oregano or dried mixed herbs
- 2 tbsp olive oil, plus extra for drizzling
- 1 large onion, finely chopped
- 450 ml/16 fl oz fish, vegetable or chicken stock
- finely grated rind and juice of 1 lime
- 2 tbsp chopped fresh coriander, plus extra to garnish
- 1 bay leaf
- 450 g/1 lb red snapper fillets, skinned and cut into chunks
- 225 g/8 oz raw prawns, peeled and deveined
- 225 g/8 oz raw squid rings
- salt and pepper
- warmed flour tortillas, to serve

Preheat the oven to 200°C/400°F/Gas Mark 6. Put the pepper quarters, skin-side up, in a roasting tin with the tomatoes, chillies and garlic. Sprinkle with the oregano and drizzle with oil. Roast in the preheated oven for 30 minutes, or until the peppers are well browned and softened.

Remove the roasted vegetables from the oven and leave to stand until cool enough to handle. Peel off the skins from the peppers, tomatoes and chillies and chop the flesh. Finely chop the garlic.

Heat the oil in a large saucepan and cook the onion, stirring frequently, for 5 minutes, or until softened. Add the peppers, tomatoes, chillies, garlic, stock, lime rind and juice, coriander, bay leaf, and salt and pepper to taste. Bring to the boil, then stir in the seafood. Reduce the heat, cover and simmer gently for 10 minutes, or until the fish and squid are just cooked through and the prawns have turned pink. Discard the bay leaf, then garnish with chopped coriander before serving accompanied by warmed flour tortillas.

moroccan fish tagine

serves 4

- 2 tbsp olive oil
- 1 large onion, finely chopped
- pinch of saffron threads
- 1/2 tsp ground cinnamon
- 1 tsp ground coriander
- 1/2 tsp ground cumin
- 1/2 tsp ground turmeric
- 200 g/7 oz canned chopped tomatoes
- 300 ml/10 fl oz fish stock
- 4 small red mullet, cleaned, boned and heads and tails removed
- 55 g/2 oz stoned green olives
- 1 tbsp chopped preserved lemon
- 3 tbsp chopped fresh coriander
- salt and pepper

Heat the olive oil in a flameproof casserole. Add the onion and cook gently over a very low heat, stirring occasionally, for 10 minutes, or until softened, but not coloured. Add the saffron, cinnamon, ground coriander, cumin and turmeric and cook for a further 30 seconds, stirring constantly.

Add the tomatoes and fish stock and stir well. Bring to the boil, reduce the heat, cover and simmer for 15 minutes. Uncover and simmer for 20–35 minutes, or until thickened.

Cut each red mullet in half, then add the fish pieces to the casserole, pushing them down under the liquid. Simmer the stew for a further 5–6 minutes, or until the fish is just cooked.

Carefully stir in the olives, preserved lemon and chopped coriander. Season to taste with salt and pepper and serve immediately.

bouillabaisse

serves 8

- 1.25 kg/2 lb 12 oz sea bass, filleted, skinned and cut into bite-sized chunks
- 1.25 kg/2 lb 12 oz red snapper, filleted, skinned and cut into bite-sized chunks
- 3 tbsp extra virgin olive oil
- grated rind of 1 orange
- 1 garlic clove, finely chopped
- pinch of saffron threads
- 2 tbsp pastis, such as Pernod
- 450 g/1 lb live mussels
- 1 large cooked crab
- 1 small fennel bulb, finely chopped
- 2 celery sticks, finely chopped
- 1 onion, finely chopped
- 1.2 litres/2 pints fish stock
- 225 g/8 oz small new potatoes, scrubbed
- 225 g/8 oz tomatoes, peeled, deseeded and chopped
- 450 g/1 lb large raw prawns, peeled and deveined
- salt and pepper

Put the fish pieces in a large bowl and add 2 tablespoons of the oil, the orange rind, garlic, saffron and pastis. Toss the fish pieces until well coated, cover and leave to marinate in the refrigerator for 30 minutes.

Meanwhile, clean the mussels by scrubbing or scraping the shells and pulling out any beards that are attached to them. Discard any with broken shells or any that refuse to close when tapped. Remove the meat from the crab, chop and reserve.

Heat the remaining oil in a large, flameproof casserole and cook the fennel, celery and onion over a low heat, stirring occasionally, for 5 minutes, or until softened. Add the stock and bring to the boil. Add the potatoes and tomatoes and cook over a medium heat for 7 minutes.

Reduce the heat and add the fish to the stew, beginning with the thickest pieces, then add the mussels, prawns and crab and simmer until the fish is opaque, the mussels have opened and the prawns have turned pink. Discard any mussels that remain closed. Season to taste with salt and pepper and serve immediately.

louisiana gumbo

serves 6

- 2 tbsp sunflower or corn oil
- 175 g/6 oz okra, trimmed and cut into 2.5-cm/1-inch pieces
- 2 onions, finely chopped
- 4 celery sticks, very finely chopped
- 1 garlic clove, finely chopped
- 2 tbsp plain flour
- 1/2 tsp sugar
- 1 tsp ground cumin
- 700 ml/1 1/4 pints fish stock
- 1 red pepper and 1 green pepper, deseeded and chopped
- 2 large tomatoes, chopped
- 350 g/12 oz large raw prawns
- 4 tbsp chopped fresh parsley
- 1 tbsp chopped fresh coriander
- dash of Tabasco sauce
- 350 g/12 oz cod or haddock fillets, skinned
- 350 g/12 oz monkfish fillet
- salt and pepper

Heat half the oil in a large, flameproof casserole, or large saucepan with tightly fitting lid, and cook the okra over a low heat, stirring frequently, for 5 minutes, or until browned. Using a slotted spoon, remove from the casserole and set aside.

Heat the remaining oil in the casserole and cook the onion and celery over a medium heat, stirring frequently, for 5 minutes, or until softened. Add the garlic and cook, stirring, for 1 minute. Sprinkle in the flour, sugar and cumin and add salt and pepper to taste. Cook, stirring constantly, for 2 minutes, then remove from the heat.

Gradually stir in the stock and bring to the boil, stirring. Return the okra to the casserole and add the peppers and tomatoes. Partially cover, reduce the heat to very low and simmer gently, stirring occasionally, for 10 minutes. Meanwhile, peel and devein the prawns and reserve.

Add the herbs and Tabasco sauce to taste. Cut the cod and monkfish into 2.5-cm/1-inch chunks, then gently stir into the stew. Stir in the prawns. Cover and simmer gently for 5 minutes, or until the fish is cooked through and the prawns have turned pink. Transfer to a large, warmed serving dish and serve.

tuna & noodle casserole

serves 4–6

- 200 g/7 oz dried ribbon egg pasta, such as tagliatelle
- 25 g/1 oz butter
- 55 g/2 oz fine fresh breadcrumbs
- 400 ml/14 fl oz canned condensed cream of mushroom soup
- 125 ml/4 fl oz milk
- 2 celery sticks, chopped
- 1 red pepper, deseeded and chopped
- 1 green pepper, deseeded and chopped
- 140 g/5 oz mature Cheddar cheese, coarsely grated
- 2 tbsp chopped fresh parsley
- 200 g/7 oz canned tuna in oil, drained and flaked
- salt and pepper

Preheat the oven to 200°C/400°F/Gas Mark 6. Bring a large saucepan of salted water to the boil. Add the pasta, return to the boil and cook for 2 minutes less than specified on the packet instructions.

Meanwhile, melt the butter in a separate small saucepan. Stir in the breadcrumbs, then remove from the heat and set aside.

Drain the pasta well and set aside. Pour the soup into the pasta saucepan over a medium heat, then stir in the milk, celery, peppers, half the cheese and all the parsley. Add the tuna and gently stir in so that the flakes don't break up. Season to taste with salt and pepper. Heat just until small bubbles appear around the edge of the mixture – do not boil.

Stir the pasta into the saucepan and use 2 forks to mix all the ingredients together. Spoon the mixture into an ovenproof dish that is also suitable for serving and spread it out.

Stir the remaining cheese into the buttered breadcrumbs, then sprinkle over the top of the pasta mixture. Bake in the preheated oven for 20–25 minutes until the topping is golden. Remove from the oven, then leave to stand for 5 minutes before serving straight from the dish.

mediterranean fish casserole

serves 6

- 2 tbsp olive oil
- 1 red onion, peeled and sliced
- 2 garlic cloves, peeled and chopped
- 2 red peppers
- 400 g/14 oz canned chopped tomatoes
- 1 tsp chopped fresh oregano or marjoram
- a few saffron strands soaked in 1 tbsp warm water for 2 minutes
- 450 g/1 lb white fish (cod, haddock or hake), skinned and boned
- 450 g/1 lb prepared squid, cut into rings
- 300 ml/10 fl oz fish or vegetable stock
- 115 g/4 oz cooked shelled prawns
- 6 cooked whole prawns in their shells
- 2 tbsp chopped fresh parsley, to garnish
- salt and pepper
- chunky bread, to serve

Heat the oil in a frying pan and fry the onion and garlic over a medium heat for 2–3 minutes until beginning to soften.

Deseed and thinly slice the peppers and add to the pan. Continue to cook over a low heat for a further 5 minutes. Add the tomatoes with the herbs and saffron and stir well.

Preheat the oven to 200°C/400°F/Gas 6. Cut the white fish into 3-cm/1¼-inch pieces and place with the squid in the casserole dish. Pour in the fried vegetable mixture and the stock, stir well and season to taste.

Cover and cook in the centre of the preheated oven for about 30 minutes, until the fish is tender and cooked. Add the prawns at the last minute and just heat through.

Serve in hot bowls garnished with the whole prawns and the parsley. Provide lots of chunky bread to mop up the casserole juices.

serves 4

- 4 tbsp lemon juice
- 6 tbsp olive oil
- 4 swordfish steaks, about 175 g/6 oz each
- 1 onion, finely chopped
- 1 garlic clove, finely chopped
- 1 tbsp plain flour
- 225 g/8 oz tomatoes, peeled, deseeded and chopped
- 1 tbsp tomato purée
- 300 ml/10 fl oz dry white wine
- salt and pepper
- fresh dill sprigs, to garnish

spanish fish in tomato sauce

Preheat the oven to 180°C/350°F/Gas Mark 4. Place the lemon juice and 4 tablespoons of the olive oil in a shallow, non-metallic dish, stir well, then season to taste with salt and pepper. Add the swordfish steaks, turning to coat thoroughly, then cover with clingfilm and leave to marinate in the refrigerator for 1 hour.

Heat the remaining oil in a flameproof casserole. Add the onion and cook over a low heat, stirring occasionally, for 10 minutes, or until golden. Add the garlic and cook, stirring frequently, for 2 minutes. Sprinkle in the flour and cook, stirring, for 1 minute, then add the tomatoes, tomato purée and wine. Bring to the boil, stirring.

Add the fish to the casserole, pushing it down under the liquid. Cover and cook in the preheated oven for 20 minutes, or until cooked through and the flesh flakes easily. Serve garnished with dill sprigs.

seafood lasagne

serves 4

- 3½ tbsp butter, plus extra for greasing
- 5 tbsp flour
- 1 tsp mustard powder
- 600 ml/1 pint milk
- 2 tbsp olive oil
- 1 onion, chopped
- 2 garlic cloves, finely chopped
- 450 g/1 lb mixed mushrooms, sliced
- 150 ml/5 fl oz white wine
- 400 g/14 oz canned chopped tomatoes
- 450 g/1 lb skinless white fish fillets
- 225 g/8 oz ready-prepared fresh scallops
- 4–6 sheets fresh lasagne
- 225 g/8 oz mozzarella cheese, chopped
- salt and pepper

Preheat the oven to 200°C/400°F/Gas Mark 6. Melt the butter in a saucepan over a low heat. Add the flour and mustard powder and stir until smooth. Simmer gently for 2 minutes without colouring. Gradually add the milk, whisking until smooth. Bring to the boil, reduce the heat and simmer for 2 minutes. Remove from the heat and reserve. Cover the surface of the sauce with clingfilm to prevent a skin forming.

Heat the oil in a frying pan. Add the onion and garlic and cook gently for 5 minutes, or until softened. Add the mushrooms and cook for 5 minutes, or until softened. Stir in the wine and boil rapidly until almost evaporated, then stir in the tomatoes. Bring to the boil, reduce the heat and simmer, covered, for 15 minutes. Season and reserve.

Cut the fish into cubes. Grease a lasagne dish, spoon half the tomato mixture over the base, top with half the fish and scallops and layer half the lasagne over the top. Pour over half the white sauce and sprinkle over half the mozzarella. Repeat these layers, finishing with sauce and mozzarella.

Bake in the preheated oven for 35–40 minutes, or until golden and the fish is cooked through. Remove from the oven and leave to stand for 10 minutes before serving.

paella del mar

serves 6

- 450 g/1 lb live mussels
- 6 squid
- 125 ml/4 fl oz olive oil
- 1 onion, chopped
- 2 garlic cloves, finely chopped
- 1 red pepper, deseeded and cut into strips
- 1 green pepper, deseeded and cut into strips
- 400 g/14 oz risotto rice
- 2 tomatoes, peeled and chopped
- 1 tbsp tomato purée
- 175 g/6 oz monkfish fillet, cut into chunks
- 175 g/6 oz red mullet fillet, cut into chunks
- 175 g/6 oz cod fillet, cut into chunks
- 500 ml/18 fl oz fish stock
- 115 g/4 oz fresh or frozen green beans, halved
- 115 g/4 oz fresh or frozen peas
- 6 canned artichoke hearts, drained
- 1/4 tsp saffron threads
- 12 raw mediterranean or tiger prawns
- salt and pepper

Clean the mussels by scrubbing or scraping the shells and pulling off any beards. Discard any with broken shells or any that refuse to close when tapped. Rinse the mussels under cold running water.

To prepare each squid, pull the pouch and tentacles apart, then remove the innards from the pouch. Slice the tentacles away from the head and discard the head. Rinse the pouch and tentacles under cold running water and slice.

Heat the oil in a paella pan or flameproof casserole. Add the onion, garlic and peppers and cook over a medium heat, stirring, for 5 minutes, or until softened. Add the squid and cook for 2 minutes. Add the rice and cook, stirring, until transparent and coated with oil.

Add the tomatoes, tomato purée and fish and cook for 3 minutes, then add the stock. Gently stir in the beans, peas, artichoke hearts and saffron and season to taste with salt and pepper.

Arrange the mussels around the edge of the pan and top the mixture with the prawns. Bring to the boil, reduce the heat and simmer, shaking the pan from time to time, for 15–20 minutes, or until the rice is tender. Discard any mussels that remain closed and serve.

rustic fish stew

makes 4–6

- 4 tbsp olive oil
- 1 onion, chopped
- 2 sticks celery, sliced
- 3 cloves garlic, sliced
- 1 tbsp smoked paprika
- 1 small pinch of saffron strands
- 150 ml/5 fl oz dry sherry
- 600 ml/1 pint chicken/fish stock
- 2 bay leaves
- 400 g/14 oz chopped tomatoes
- 550 g /1¼ lb waxy potatoes, peeled and cut into quarters
- salt and pepper
- 2 red peppers, deseeded and sliced
- 1.5 kg/3 lb mixed seafood (shelled, deveined prawns, squid rings, mussels, cod, monkfish and salmon, cut into bite-sized pieces)
- 1–2 tbsp of chopped fresh flat-leaf parsley, to garnish
- 1 lemon, finely grated
- extra virgin olive oil, for drizzling

Heat the oil in a medium-sized saucepan and fry the onion, celery and garlic over a medium heat for 2–3 minutes until beginning to soften.

Add the smoked paprika and saffron strands and cook for a further minute, then add the sherry and reduce by half.

Add the stock, bay leaves, tomatoes and potatoes, season with salt and pepper and cook for 10 minutes, or until the potatoes are almost cooked. Add the red pepper and cook for an additional 10 minutes.

If using mussels, clean them by scrubbing or scraping the shells and pulling off any beards. Discard any with broken shells or any that refuse to close when tapped. Rinse the mussels under cold running water. Carefully add the seafood to the saucepan, stirring only once or twice. Place the lid on the pan and cook for 8–10 minutes or until the seafood is cooked through. Discard any mussels that remain closed, turn off the heat and leave to stand for 2 minutes.

Serve the stew in a large bowl, sprinkled with the chopped parsley and grated lemon. Season with salt and pepper and drizzle with extra virgin olive oil.

4

Vegetable Casseroles

serves 8

1 red cabbage, about 750 g/ 1 lb 10 oz

2 onions, peeled and finely sliced

1 garlic clove, peeled and chopped

2 small cooking apples, peeled, cored and sliced

2 tbsp muscovado sugar

1/2 tsp ground cinnamon

whole nutmeg, for grating

2 tbsp red wine vinegar

zest and juice of 1 orange

salt and pepper

2 tbsp redcurrant jelly

red cabbage casserole

Preheat the oven to 150°C/300°F/Gas 2. Cut the cabbage into quarters and remove the centre stalk. Shred finely.

In the casserole dish, layer up the red cabbage, onions, garlic and apples. Sprinkle over the sugar and cinnamon and grate a quarter of the nutmeg over the top.

Pour over the wine vinegar and orange juice and scatter over the orange zest.

Stir well and season. The dish will be quite full but the volume of the cabbage will reduce during cooking.

Cook in the centre of the preheated oven for 1–1 1/2 hours, stirring from time to time. If you prefer, you can cook it more quickly in a flameproof casserole dish on the top of the stove over a medium heat for 8–10 minutes until the cabbage is just tender. The stove way leaves the cabbage more crunchy.

Stir in the redcurrant jelly, and adjust the seasoning if necessary. Serve hot.

vegetable chilli

serves 4

- 1 aubergine, cut into 2.5-cm/1-inch slices
- 1 tbsp olive oil, plus extra for brushing
- 1 large red or yellow onion, finely chopped
- 2 red or yellow peppers, deseeded and finely chopped
- 3–4 garlic cloves, finely chopped or crushed
- 800 g/1 lb 12 oz canned chopped tomatoes
- 1 tbsp mild chilli powder
- 1/2 tsp ground cumin
- 1/2 tsp dried oregano
- salt and pepper
- 2 small courgettes, quartered lengthways and sliced
- 400 g/14 oz canned kidney beans, drained and rinsed
- 450 ml/16 fl oz water
- 1 tbsp tomato purée
- 6 spring onions, finely chopped
- 115 g/4 oz Cheddar cheese, grated
- crusty bread, to serve

Brush the aubergine slices on one side with olive oil. Heat half the oil in a large, heavy-based frying pan. Add the aubergine slices, oiled-side up, and cook over a medium heat for 5–6 minutes, or until browned on one side. Turn the slices over, cook on the other side until browned and transfer to a plate. Cut into bite-sized pieces and reserve.

Heat the remaining oil in a large saucepan over a medium heat. Add the chopped onion and peppers to the saucepan and cook, stirring occasionally, for 3–4 minutes, or until the onion is just softened, but not browned. Add the garlic and cook for a further 2–3 minutes, or until the onion just begins to colour.

Add the tomatoes, chilli powder, cumin and oregano. Season to taste with salt and pepper. Bring just to the boil, reduce the heat, cover and simmer gently for 15 minutes.

Add the sliced courgettes, aubergine pieces and kidney beans. Stir in the water and tomato purée. Return to the boil, then cover the saucepan and simmer for a further 45 minutes, or until the vegetables are tender. Taste and adjust the seasoning, if necessary.

Ladle into warmed bowls and top with spring onions and cheese. Serve with crusty bread.

cold weather vegetable casserole

serves 4

- 50 g/2 oz butter
- 2 leeks, sliced
- 2 carrots, sliced
- 2 potatoes, cut into bite-sized pieces
- 1 swede, cut into bite-sized pieces
- 2 courgettes, sliced
- 1 fennel bulb, halved and sliced
- 2 tbsp plain flour
- 425 g/15 oz canned butter beans
- 450 ml/ 16 fl oz vegetable stock
- 2 tbsp tomato puree
- 1 tsp dried thyme
- 2 bay leaves
- salt and pepper

for the dumplings

- 115 g/4 oz self-raising flour
- pinch of salt
- 55 g/2 oz suet
- 2 tbsp chopped fresh parsley
- 4 tbsp water

Melt the butter in a large frying pan over low heat. Add the leeks, carrots, potatoes, swede, courgettes and fennel and cook, stirring occasionally for 10 minutes. Stir in the flour and cook, stirring constantly for 1 minute. Stir in the can juices from the beans, the stock, tomato puree, thyme and bay leaves and season to taste with salt and pepper. Bring to the boil, stirring constantly, then cover and simmer for 10 minutes.

To make the dumplings sift the flour and salt together in a bowl, add the suet and mix well. Stir in the parsley and then pour in enough of the water to form a firm but soft dough. Break the dough into 8 pieces and roll them into round dumplings (you might need some flour on your hands for this).

Add the butter beans and the dumplings to the pan, pushing them down under the liquid. Cover and simmer for a further 30 minutes or until the dumplings have doubled in size.

Remove and discard the bay leaves and serve the stew and dumplings piping hot.

serves 4

- 4 garlic cloves
- 1 small acorn squash
- 1 red onion, sliced
- 2 leeks, sliced
- 1 aubergine, sliced
- 1 small celeriac, diced
- 2 turnips, sliced
- 2 plum tomatoes, chopped
- 1 carrot, sliced
- 1 courgette, sliced
- 2 red peppers
- 1 fennel bulb, sliced
- 175 g/6 oz chard
- 2 bay leaves
- 1/2 tsp fennel seeds
- 1/2 tsp chilli powder
- pinch each of dried thyme, dried oregano and sugar
- 125 ml/4 fl oz extra virgin olive oil
- 225 ml/8 fl oz vegetable stock
- 25 g/1 oz fresh basil leaves, torn
- 4 tbsp chopped fresh parsley
- salt and pepper
- 2 tbsp freshly grated Parmesan cheese, to serve

Italian vegetable stew

Finely chop the garlic and dice the squash. Put them in a large, heavy-based saucepan with a tight-fitting lid. Add the onion, leeks, aubergine, celeriac, turnips, tomatoes, carrot, courgette, red peppers, fennel, chard, bay leaves, fennel seeds, chilli powder, thyme, oregano, sugar, oil, stock and half the basil in a large, heavy-based saucepan. Mix together well, then bring to the boil.

Reduce the heat, cover and simmer for 30 minutes, or until all the vegetables are tender.

Sprinkle in the remaining basil and the parsley and season to taste with salt and pepper. Serve immediately, sprinkled with the cheese.

black bean casserole

serves 4

- 6 Chinese dried mushrooms
- 275 g/9½ oz firm tofu
- 3 tbsp vegetable oil
- 1 carrot, cut into thin strips
- 125 g/4½ oz mangetout
- 125 g/4½ oz baby sweetcorn cobs, halved lengthways
- 225 g/8 oz canned sliced bamboo shoots, drained
- 1 red pepper, deseeded and cut into chunks
- 125 g/4½ oz Chinese leaves, shredded
- 1 tbsp soy sauce
- 1 tbsp black bean sauce
- 1 tsp sugar
- salt and pepper
- 1 tsp cornflour
- vegetable oil, for deep-frying
- 250 g/9 oz Chinese rice noodles

Soak the dried mushrooms in a bowl of warm water for 20–25 minutes. Drain and squeeze out the excess water, reserving the liquid. Remove the tough centres and slice the mushrooms thinly.

Cut the tofu into cubes, then boil in a pan of lightly salted water for 2–3 minutes to firm up, and drain.

Heat half the vegetable oil in a saucepan. Add the tofu and fry until lightly browned. Remove and drain on kitchen paper.

Add the remaining vegetable oil and stir-fry the mushrooms, carrot, mangetout, baby sweetcorn, bamboo shoots and pepper for 2–3 minutes. Add the Chinese leaves and tofu, and continue to stir-fry for a further 2 minutes.

Stir in the soy and black bean sauces and the sugar, and season with a little salt. Add 6 tablespoons of the reserved mushroom liquid mixed with the cornflour. Bring to the boil, reduce the heat, cover and braise for about 2–3 minutes, until the sauce thickens slightly.

Heat the oil for deep-frying in a large pan. Deep-fry the noodles, in batches, until puffed up and lightly golden. Drain and serve with the casserole.

serves 6

- 225 g/8 oz dried haricot beans, soaked overnight and drained
- 6 tbsp olive oil
- 2 large onions, sliced
- 2 garlic cloves, chopped
- 2 bay leaves
- 1 tsp dried oregano
- 1 tsp dried thyme
- 5 tbsp red wine
- 2 tbsp tomato purée
- 850 ml/1½ pints vegetable stock
- 225 g/8 oz dried penne, or other short pasta shapes
- 2 celery sticks, sliced
- 1 fennel bulb, sliced
- 125 g/4½ oz mushrooms, sliced
- 225 g/8 oz tomatoes, sliced
- 1 tsp dark muscovado sugar
- 50 g/1¾ oz dried white breadcrumbs
- salt and pepper
- salad leaves and crusty bread, to serve

pasta & bean casserole

Place the beans in a saucepan, cover with water and bring to the boil. Boil rapidly for 20 minutes, then drain.

Place the beans in a large flameproof casserole, stir in 5 tablespoons of the olive oil, the onions, garlic, bay leaves, herbs, wine and tomato purée and pour in the vegetable stock.

Bring to the boil, then cover the casserole and bake in a preheated oven, 180°C/350°F/Gas Mark 4, for 2 hours.

Towards the end of the cooking time, bring a large saucepan of lightly salted water to the boil, add the pasta and the remaining oil, and cook for 3 minutes. Drain and set aside.

Remove the casserole from the oven and add the pasta, celery, fennel, mushrooms and tomatoes and season to taste with salt and pepper.

Stir in the sugar and sprinkle over the breadcrumbs. Cover the casserole again, return to the oven and continue cooking for 1 hour. Serve hot with salad leaves and crusty bread.

spring stew

serves 4

- 225 g/8 oz dried haricot beans
- 2 tbsp olive oil
- 4–8 baby onions, halved
- 2 celery sticks, cut into 5-mm/1/4-inch slices
- 225 g/8 oz baby carrots, scrubbed and halved if large
- 300 g/10 1/2 oz new potatoes, scrubbed and halved, or quartered if large
- 850 ml–1.2 litres/1 1/2–2 pints vegetable stock
- 1 fresh bouquet garni
- 1 1/2–2 tbsp light soy sauce
- 85 g/3 oz baby sweetcorn
- 115 g/4 oz frozen or shelled fresh broad beans, thawed if frozen
- 1/2–1 savoy or spring (Primo) cabbage, about 225 g/8 oz
- 1 1/2 tbsp cornflour
- 2 tbsp cold water
- salt and pepper
- 55–85 g/2–3 oz Parmesan or mature Cheddar cheese, grated, to serve

Pick over the haricot beans, rinse thoroughly, drain and put in a large bowl. Cover with plenty of cold water and leave to soak overnight. The next day, drain, put in a saucepan and cover with cold water. Bring to the boil and boil rapidly for 10 minutes, then drain and set aside.

Heat the oil in a large, heavy-based saucepan, with a tight-fitting lid, and cook the vegetables, stirring frequently, for 5 minutes, or until softened. Add the stock, drained beans, bouquet garni and soy sauce, then bring to the boil. Reduce the heat, cover and simmer for 12 minutes.

Add the baby sweetcorn and broad beans and season to taste with salt and pepper. Simmer for a further 3 minutes.

Meanwhile, discard the outer leaves and hard central core from the cabbage and shred the leaves. Add to the saucepan and simmer for a further 3–5 minutes, or until all the vegetables are tender.

Blend the cornflour with the water, stir into the saucepan and cook, stirring, for 4–6 minutes, or until the liquid has thickened. Serve the cheese separately, for stirring into the stew.

vegetable & lentil casserole

serves 4

- 10 cloves
- 1 onion, peeled but kept whole
- 225 g/8 oz Puy or green lentils
- 1 bay leaf
- 1.5 litres/2¾ pints vegetable stock
- 2 leeks, sliced
- 2 potatoes, diced
- 2 carrots, chopped
- 3 courgettes, sliced
- 1 celery stick, chopped
- 1 red pepper, deseeded and chopped
- salt and pepper
- 1 tbsp lemon juice

Preheat the oven to 180°C/350°F/Gas Mark 4. Press the cloves into the onion. Put the lentils into a large casserole, add the onion and bay leaf and pour in the stock. Cover and cook in the preheated oven for 1 hour.

Remove the onion and discard the cloves. Slice the onion and return it to the casserole with the vegetables. Stir thoroughly and season to taste with salt and pepper. Cover and return to the oven for 1 hour.

Discard the bay leaf. Stir in the lemon juice and serve straight from the casserole.

layered vegetable casserole

serves 4

- 1 tbsp olive oil, for brushing
- 680 g/1 lb 8 oz potatoes, peeled and thinly sliced
- 2 leeks, trimmed and sliced
- 2 beef tomatoes, sliced
- 8 fresh basil leaves
- 1 garlic clove, finely chopped
- 150 ml/5 fl oz vegetable stock
- salt and pepper

Preheat the oven to 180°C/350°F/Gas Mark 4. Brush a large flameproof casserole with a little of the olive oil.

Place a layer of potato slices in the bottom of the casserole and cover with a layer of leeks. Top with a layer of tomato slices. Repeat these layers until all the vegetables are used up, ending with a layer of potatoes. Stir the chopped garlic into the vegetable stock and season to taste with salt and pepper. Pour the stock over the vegetables and brush the top with the remaining oil.

Bake in the centre of the preheated oven for 1½ hours, or until the vegetables are tender and the topping is golden and brown. Serve immediately.

serves 4

15 g/½ oz sun-dried tomatoes, chopped

225 g/8 oz Puy lentils

600 ml/1 pint cold water

2 tbsp olive oil

½–1 tsp crushed dried chillies

2–3 garlic cloves, chopped

1 large onion, cut into small wedges

1 small celeriac, cut into small chunks

225 g/8 oz carrots, sliced

225 g/8 oz new potatoes, scrubbed and cut into chunks

1 small acorn squash, deseeded, peeled and cut into small chunks, about 225 g/8 oz prepared weight

2 tbsp tomato purée

300 ml/10 fl oz vegetable stock

1–2 tsp hot paprika

few fresh sprigs of thyme

450 g/1 lb ripe tomatoes

soured cream and crusty bread, to serve

vegetable goulash

Put the sun-dried tomatoes in a small heatproof bowl, cover with almost boiling water and leave to soak for 15–20 minutes. Drain, reserving the soaking liquid. Meanwhile, rinse and drain the lentils, and put them in a saucepan with the cold water and bring to the boil. Reduce the heat, cover and simmer for 15 minutes. Drain and set aside.

Heat the oil in a large, heavy-based saucepan, with a tight-fitting lid, and cook the chillies, garlic and vegetables, stirring frequently, for 5–8 minutes until softened. Blend the tomato purée with a little of the stock in a jug and pour over the vegetable mixture, then add the remaining stock, lentils, the sun-dried tomatoes and their soaking liquid, and the paprika and thyme.

Bring to the boil, then reduce the heat, cover and simmer for 15 minutes. Add the fresh tomatoes and simmer for a further 15 minutes, or until the vegetables and lentils are tender. Serve topped with spoonfuls of soured cream, accompanied by crusty bread.